DOODLE THROUGH THE BIBLE FOR KIDS

JONNY HAWKINS

HARVEST HOUSE PUBLISHERS
EUGENE, OREGON

DOODLE THROUGH THE BIBLE FOR KIDS
Copyright © 2016 Jonny Hawkins
Published by Harvest House Publishers
Eugene, Oregon 97402
www.harvesthousepublishers.com

ISBN 978-0-7369-6520-0 (pbk.)

Printed in the United States of America

16 17 18 19 20 21 22 23 24 / VP-CD / 10 9 8 7 6 5 4 3 2 1

Doodles

AND WHAT ON EARTH IS THERE?

WHAT WAS GOD'S AMAZINGLY BRIGHT IDEA?

DOODLE IT!

DOODLE OTHER SOURCES OF LIGHT.

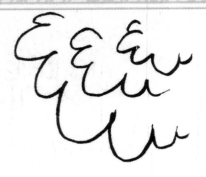

WHAT KINDS OF FUN AND AMAZING PLANTS
AND ANIMALS COULD HAVE BEEN IN
THE GARDEN?

LET YOUR IMAGINATION (AND PENCIL) RUN WILD!

WHAT IS THE
GIRAFFE BUILDING?
A GIROOF ?

IF THE ANIMALS COULD HAVE HELPED BUILD THE ARK,
WHAT WOULD THEY HAVE DONE? NOAH WAY TO DOODLE IT?

WHO WOULD HELP THE WOODPECKER DRILL AND THE
ELEPHANT MEASURE (IN ELE-FEET) AND SAW? LET US SEE!

DOODLE JOSEPH'S EYE-POPPING COAT OF MANY COLORS.

DOODLE THE EXPRESSION AND HEAD OF ONE OF JOE'S FRUSTRATED BROS.

DOODLE A PIT THAT SURROUNDS JOSEPH. WHAT WOULD YOU BE FEELING?

LATER, JOSEPH WAS FALSELY ACCUSED BY POTIPHAR'S WIFE. HAVE YOU EVER BEEN FALSELY ACCUSED? WHEN?

WHAT ELSE MIGHT BE IN HIS DUNGEON PRISON? DOODLE IT. LATER, GOD RESTORED JOSEPH.

DOODLE A STAFF FOR MOSES'S HAND.

FINISH THE WALLS OF WATER AND AMAZING LIFE WITHIN THEM.

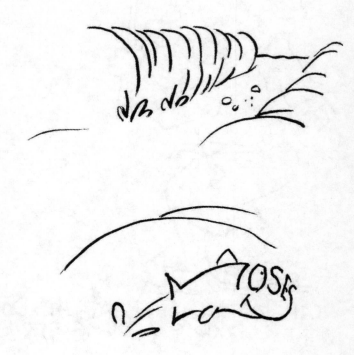

CAN YOU SPELL OUT "MIRACLE"
WITH FISH AND DROPS OF WATER? LET'S SEA.

Balaam's Donkey

ANGRY BALAAM BEATS HIS DONKEY.
DOODLE A DUMB-STRUCK BEAST.

WOW. YOU REALLY KNOW HOW TO DRIVE A STICK.

SUDDENLY, THE DONKEY TALKED! WHAT DID IT REALLY SAY? WHAT DID IT SILLY SAY?

DOODLE WHAT'S BLOCKING THE ROAD THAT BALAAM CAN'T SEE.

STOP! THERE'S A ROADBLOCK!

PEN THE TAIL ON THE DONKEY... AND DON'T FORGET HIS HEAD!

FINISH THE FAMILY.

UNVEIL DAD'S TEACHINGS.
WHAT'S ON THE SCROLL?

THE LIVING WORD... LIVING THE WORD.

WHAT IS HE PAINTING ON THE DOORPOSTS?

REDRAW GOLIATH SWITCHING OUT THE 17 THINGS THAT DON'T BELONG.

DOODLE YOURSELF BEING STRONG WHILE FACING YOUR GIANTS.

Repent

WHAT <u>4</u> QUALITIES DOES ONE NEED TO RECEIVE GOD'S BLESSING?

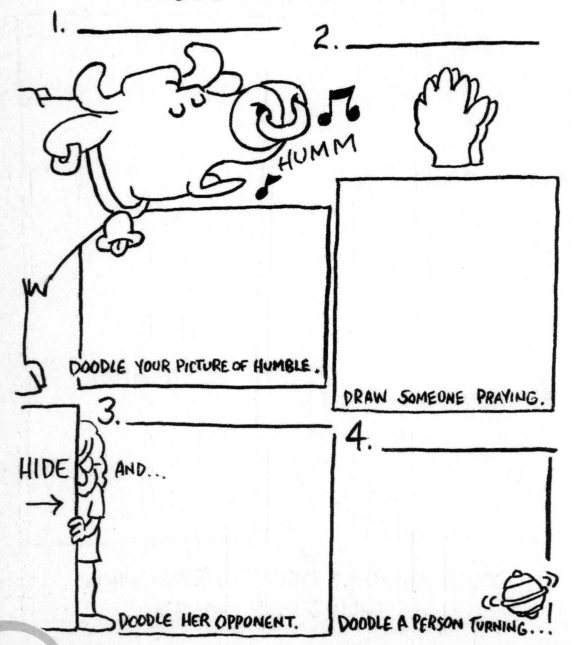

1. _____

2. _____

HUMM

DOODLE YOUR PICTURE OF HUMBLE.

DRAW SOMEONE PRAYING.

3. _____

HIDE → AND...

DOODLE HER OPPONENT.

4. _____

DOODLE A PERSON TURNING...

WHAT <u>3</u> WAYS WILL GOD RESPOND?

1. _____   2. _____

HOW DOES HE DO IT?

HOW DO YOU SEE HIM HEAR?

PICTURE HOW GOD HEALS OUR LAND.

Rx

3. _____

God's Glory

DRAW HIS NAME IN THE HEAVENS USING CLOUDS, BIRDS, RAINBOW, ETC.

WHAT IS THIS STAR DECLARING ABOUT GOD'S POWER?

WHAT IS THIS BUTTERFLY GIVING A SHOUT-OUT ABOUT GOD'S BEAUTY?

WHY IS THIS CLOUD SO LOUD AND PROUD ABOUT GOD'S ROYALTY?

MAYBE BECAUSE IT'S A REIGN CLOUD!

WHY IS THIS MOON LUNAR ABOUT GOD?

Faithfulness

FINISH THE RAINBOW. DOODLE OTHER THINGS
IN THE SKY THAT SHOW GOD'S LOVE. A DOVE?

Out of the Mud

STICK-IN-THE-MUD LIVES HERE

TAKE YOUR PIG PEN AND DOODLE SOME MUD SCULPTURES ON THIS HOG IN A BOG.

DOODLE A MONSTER MADE OF MUD

DRAW SOMEONE'S FEET SET UPON THE ROCK. ARE THEY YOURS?

DOODLE THE REST OF
THE DEER FROM "AS
THE DEER PANTS..."

WHAT DO PEOPLE
USE TO TRY TO QUENCH
THEIR THIRST?
DEW-DLE THEM!

WHAT MIGHT A THIRSTY SOUL LOOK LIKE?

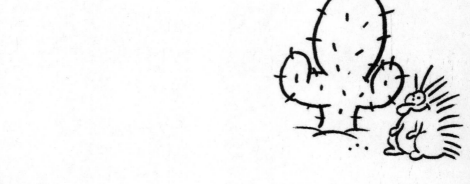

HOW
DID YOU
LOOK

AFTER
GOD
REFRESHED
YOU?

TO WHOM IS HE SPEAKING AND
WHAT IS HE SAYING?

Unfailing Love

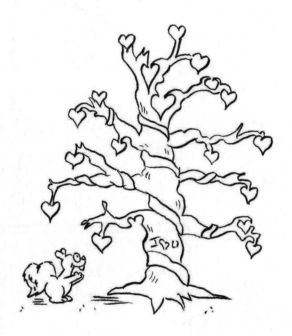

THE WRITER SAYS HE IS "LIKE AN OLIVE TREE FLOURISHING IN THE HOUSE OF GOD." THIS IS AN "I LOVE..." TREE. DRAW A GREAT HOUSE AROUND IT.

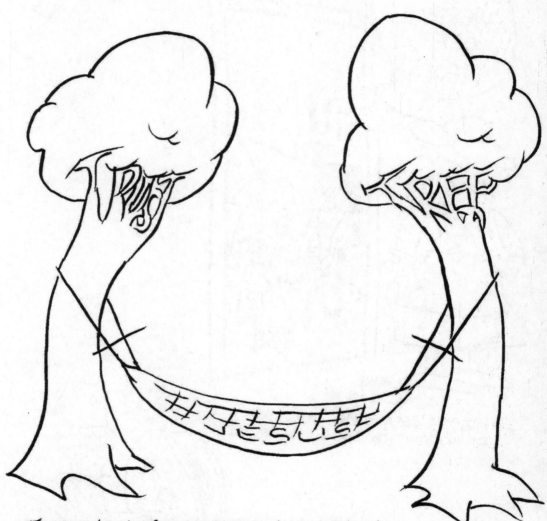

TRUSTING IN GOD'S UNFAILING LOVE IS
LIKE YOU RESTING IN THE HAMMOCK. DOODLE YOU!
HOW DOES GOD SHOW YOU LOVE?

Worship

DOODLE MORE PEOPLE UNDER THE STEEPLE MAKING A JOYFUL NOISE.

DOODLE OTHER CREATURES MAKING A JOYFUL NOISE TO THEIR CREATOR.

Praise Him

DOODLE PEOPLE PRAISING GOD IN HIS SANG-TUARY...
AND DOODLE THE REST OF THE SANCTUARY.

WHAT IS COMING OUT OF HIS INSTRUMENT?

DOODLE AN UNUSUAL INSTRUMENT ONE COULD USE TO PRAISE GOD!

TAKE NOTE... DOODLE
JOYFUL NOISEMAKERS OUT OF
NOTES!

WHAT OTHER BEACH CREATURES OR INSTRU-ANIMALS
CAN YOU DOO-TA-DOODLE? GUITARFISH?
CELLO FISH?

Wisdom

HOW DO YOU GET WISDOM?

OWL BET YOU ← CAN'T DOODLE IT!

WRITE SOMETHING VALUABLE YOU HAVE LEARNED FROM GOD... ON THESE PEARLS.

WE OFTEN SHOWCASE SOMETHING WE VALUE. DRAW WISDOM ON DISPLAY. (PERHAPS SOMEONE YOU KNOW WHO IS WISE)

WHAT WILL WISDOM PLACE ON YOUR HEAD? DRAW THIS CROWNING ACHIEVEMENT!

THIS LITTLE BOY
TAKES CARE OF HIS
BIG PET.

HOW DO YOU
CARE FOR YOUR
BEAST?
DOODLE IT!

FINISH THESE PETS AND ADD A BIRD
AT THE TOP.   WHAT ARE THEY EATING?

Grandparents

WHAT ARE KIDS
TO THEIR GRANDPARENTS?

DOODLE OTHER ROYAL
OLDER ONES AND KIDS!

DOODLE SOMETHING GRAND YOU DO WITH YOUR GRANDPARENTS.

Doodle Through the Bible for Kids

TAKE FEATURES FROM EACH OF THESE SONS...

...AND DOODLE THEIR DAD.

DRAW WHY YOU ARE PROUD OF YOUR POP!
DADDLE... I MEAN DOODLE IT!

FINISH CONSTRUCTING
THIS STRONG TOWER
USING THE LORD'S NAME
ON IT.

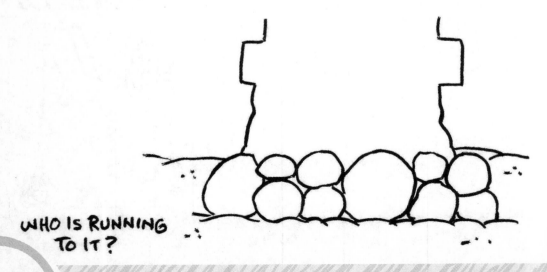

WHO IS RUNNING
TO IT?

DOODLE A POLICE OFFICER, A SECURITY GUARD, AN ARMY...
OR JUST A STRONG MAN... PROTECTING THIS BABY.

DOODLE A TIME GOD KEPT YOU SAFE!

DOODLE AN ENGINEER TRAINING A CHILD.   STAY ON TRACK AND FINISH THE TRAIN.

DOODLE A WAY DAD HAS TRAINED YOU. CHOO CHOOSE WISELY.

DOODLE THIS PERSON IN THREE STAGES OF LIFE LEARNING ABOUT GOD'S LOVE.

1)

2)

3)

Eternal Things

THESE ONCE-SHARP BLADES OF GRASS ARE DULL AND WITHERED! WHAT HAPPENED?!

DOODLE A FLOWER FADING... THEN BITING THE DUST.

FINISH THIS PICTURE OF A BUILDING FIRE
WITH JUST THE WORD OF GOD ESCAPING UNBURNED.

DRAW A FALLEN TOWER. WHAT ONE THING STANDS?

FINISH
THE
EAGLE.

DOODLE YOURSELF WITH WINGS... SOARING.

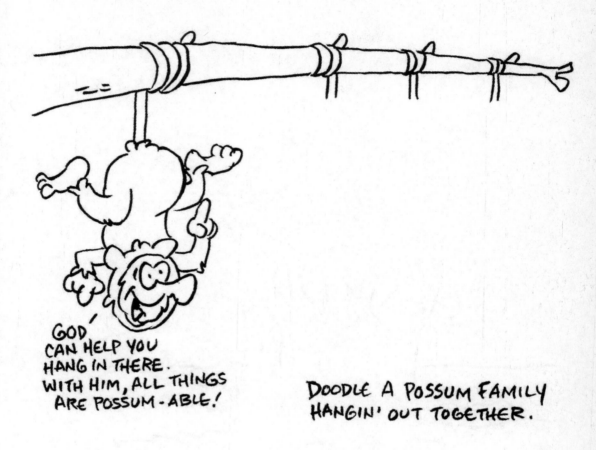

GOD
CAN HELP YOU
HANG IN THERE.
WITH HIM, ALL THINGS
ARE POSSUM-ABLE!

DOODLE A POSSUM FAMILY
HANGIN' OUT TOGETHER.

PICTURE HOW HE HELPS YOU... HANG IN THERE!

Trust in the Lord

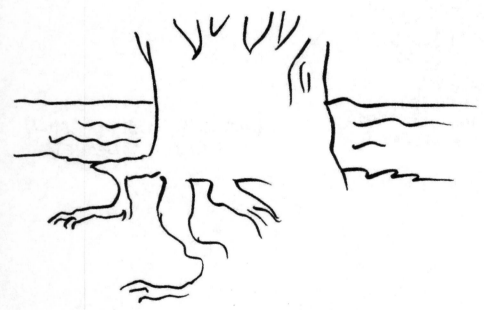

DOODLE A BIG BEAUTIFUL TREE. DOODLE YOUR FAMILY IN IT. DOODLE BIG ROOTS UNDER THE RIVER. I'M ROOTING FOR YOU! FINISH THE RIVER AND SCENERY.

FINISH THE OTHER BEAVER. DOODLE OTHER
RIVER CRITTERS AND WILDLIFE.

THIS CAT IS SEEKING LONG AND HARD FOR A MOUSE.
DOODLE MICE HIDING THROUGHOUT THE PICTURE.

FINISH THE HELICOPTER. WHO IS THE PILOT, AND DID
HE FIND THE LOST PERSON?
WHEN DO WE FIND GOD? _____

The Fiery Furnace

DOODLE THE OLD JOKE –
MY SHACK, YOUR SHACK, AND
A BUNGALOW!

HERE'S SHADRACH NOW! WHERE ARE
THE OTHER TWO? WHAT DID THEY NOT DO?

DOODLE FIRE IN THE FURNACE.
WHO'S ABOUT TO ENTER...
AND BE ON FIRE FOR GOD?

WHAT DOES KING NEB SEE WHEN HE LOOKS INTO THE FURNACE?!
HOW MANY PEOPLE? WERE THEY BURNED? DRAW HIS EXPRESSION!

DANIEL WOULD PRAY THREE TIMES A DAY.

DOODLE A PLACE YOU OFTEN PRAY.

WHAT DID THE HANDWRITING ON THE WALL SAY? DOODLE IT!

HERE, KITTY KITTY!

FINISH THE LION AND WHO SHUT ITS MOUTH? I'M NOT LION.

DRAW A TIME YOU NEEDED GOD'S HELP... WITH AN ANIMAL.

Jonah

DOODLE A STORM AND A
RAGING SEA.

WHERE DID GOD
TELL JONAH TO GO?

_____

WHERE DID HE
DECIDE TO GO?

_____

GO OVERBOARD AND FINISH THE SHIP JONAH BOARDED
TO TARSHISH.

JONAH CAN'T STOMACH HIS SITUATION AND CALLS OUT TO GOD, PROMISING HE'LL GO WHERE HE'S TOLD.

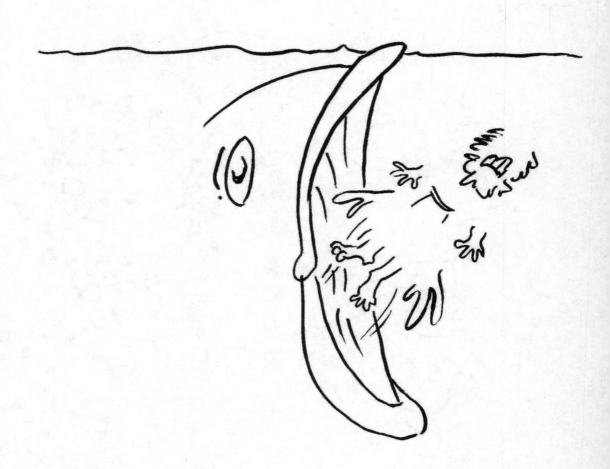

FINISH A FISHY-LOOKING JONAH AND THE GREAT FISH WHO IS EJECTING HIM TO SHORE.

DOODLE DEER ATOP THE CLIFF MOUNTS AND A FEW OTHERS ON THE SIDE.

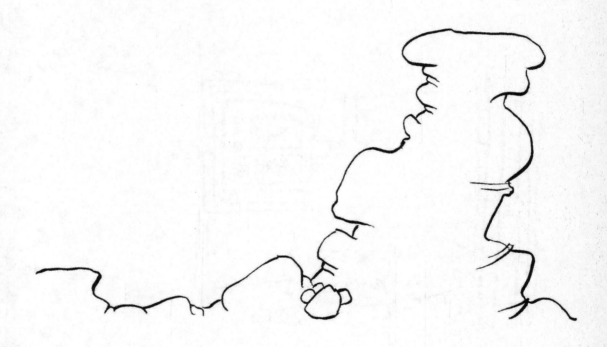

SPELL OUT "SOVEREIGN LORD" IN CLIFF BOULDERS.
EXCEPT FOR THE ROCKS, IT'S NOT HARD. I DID THE "S" FOR YOU.

DON'T STALL. QUICKLY DRAW 1) A SICK COW 2) A HEALTHY
CALF - FAT AND HAPPY - SKIPPING ABOUT IN THE SUN.
(NO DECALF, GIVE IT ENERGY!)

3) ADD WINGS (OF HEALING) TO THE SUN. WRITE THE WORD "REVERENCE" IN CLOUD LETTERS AND "GOD" INSIDE THOSE.

God Provides

DRAW WORRY WARTS ON
THE FROG.

FINISH THIS
NERVOUS TICK.

DRAW YOURSELF CALM ... LIKE THIS CLAM.

WHAT FOOD HAS GOD PROVIDED FOR YOU TODAY?

WHAT DRINK?

CRUMMY?   YUMMY?

SLOPPY?   SLURPY?

DRAW A TURTLE-NECK FOR CROC...

DESIGN HER WOOL...
FOR EWE... BY YOU.

...AND CROCS FOR TURTLE.

Bird's-Eye View

FILL THE FRIENDLY SKIES
WITH THINGS THAT GOD MAKES
FLY!

HOW DOES GOD FEED THE BIRDS?

DRAW A WORM AND BUG BUFFET!

OH, GOD - HELP ME TO BE A BIRDWATCHER SO I CAN BE REMINDED OF HOW YOU CARE FOR EVERY LITTLE CREATURE. YOU GIVE ME FOOD AND CLOTHES TOO, WHICH MAKES US "BIRDS OF A FEATHER," BUT YOU CARE SO MUCH MORE FOR YOUR CHILDREN THAT IT SHOULD MAKE ME A "BIRD BRAIN," AND NOT WORRY, BUT SOAR!

WHO'S WATCHING?

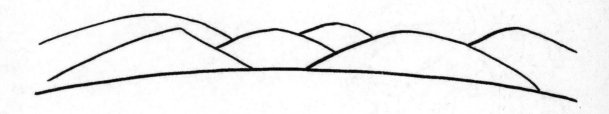

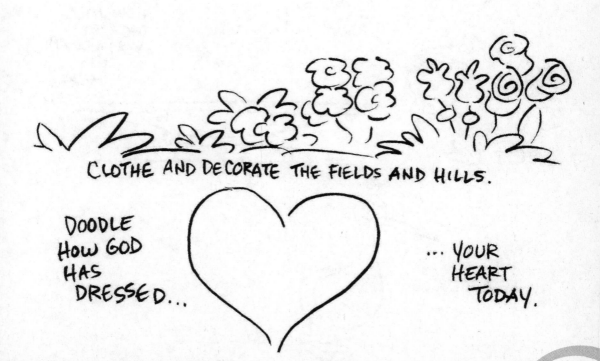

CLOTHE AND DECORATE THE FIELDS AND HILLS.

DOODLE HOW GOD HAS DRESSED...

... YOUR HEART TODAY.

WHAT IS THE LION'S "MANE" COURSE OF FOOD?

HOW WILL THE BIRD WASH DOWN HIS MEAL?

DRESS THE PEACOCK.

WHAT DOES HE SEEK?

SEEK AND FIND THE HIDDEN LETTERS, WRITING THEM OUT
IN THE ORDER IN WHICH FOUND.

WHAT ARE
YOU
SEEKING?

WHAT WAS IN THE
BOY'S LUNCH? NO LOAFING!
DOODLE IT!

DRAWING A CROWD...

CAN YOU MAKE A BREAD PERSON? WOULD LOAVE
TO SEE IT!

JESUS COULD DIVIDE, ADD, OR MULTIPLY!
BECAUSE HE'S THE RULER!

DOODLE A TIME YOU WERE MIRACULOUSLY FED BY GOD!

WHAT FOOD,
DUDE, DO YOU
THANK GOD FOR?
DOODLE IT!
→

DRAW FISH AND
BREAD POPPING
OUT OF THIS
DISCIPLE'S TUNIC!
(WHAT? TUNIC FISH SANDWICHES?!)

THIS IS WHAT IT WOULD HAVE LOOKED LIKE IF PETER WALKED ON WATER... IN WINTER AND UP NORTH.

DOODLE WHAT IT REALLY LOOKED LIKE!

DOODLE PETER SINKING AND NEEDING A HAND FROM JESUS.

DOODLE THE REST OF THE BOAT AROUND JESUS AND PETER.

THE INITIALS FOR WALKING ON WATER... IS W.O.W !
CAN YOU DOODLE A WOW MOMENT IN YOUR LIFE WITH JESUS ?

Jesus & Children

FINISH THE OTHER HALF OF THIS HALF-MAD DISCIPLE. WHAT IS HE SAYING?

DOODLE OTHER HAPPY CHILDREN COMING TO JESUS!

DOODLE YOU AS A CHILD COMING TO JESUS.

Forgiving Others

FINISH THE ELEPHANT.

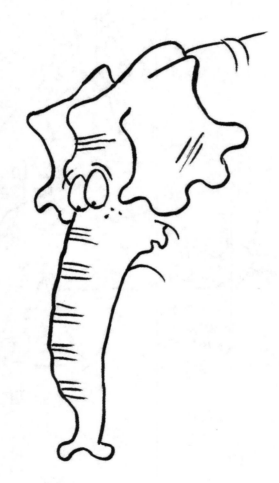

TO WHOM OR WHAT IS ELEPHANT FORGIVING?
(AND FORGETTING?) HMM... THAT WOULD BE HARD!

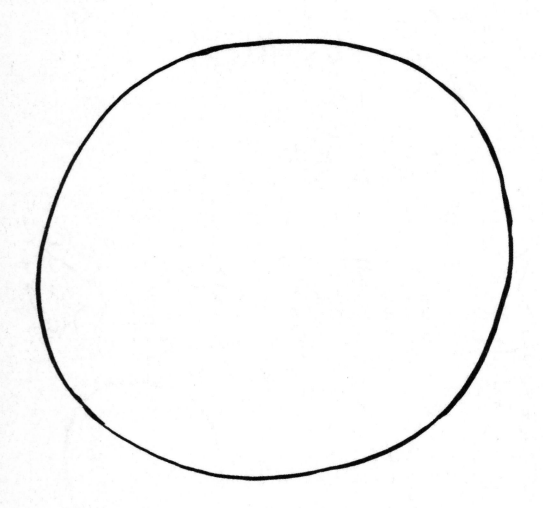

FOR GOD SO LOVED THE WORLD...

WHAT DOES THAT LOOK LIKE TO YOU?

HAVE YOU EVER HAD TO
GIVE UP SOMETHING YOU
LOVED?

WHAT WAS
IT?
⇩

WHAT DOES A PERSON
RECEIVE WHEN THEY BELIEVE?
DOODLE IT! ↓

believe box

HAVE YOU EVER BELIEVED IN JESUS?
WHEN DID YOU DECIDE TO?

The Good Shepherd

NICEST VOICE EVER HERD...

DOODLE MORE SHEEP.

FINISH THIS WOLF IN SHEEP'S CLOTHING.

WHAT WOLVES MUST WE BE AWARE OF?

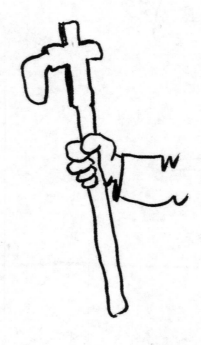

DOODLE THE GOOD SHEPHERD PROTECTING
HIS SHEEP. TRUSTWORTHY STAFF?

DOODLE WHO JESUS IS TALKING TO.

I AM THE...

(BUBBLE LETTERS)

(3D LETTERS)

(PUT IT ON CEREAL BOX)

AND THE

DOODLE HOW ONE GETS TO THE FATHER.

THIS FATHER WANTS TO SPEND TIME WITH HIS SON. COMPLETE THE PICTURE.

HOW DO YOU GET TO KNOW YOUR HEAVENLY FATHER?

In the Vine

WHAT PET WOULD NOT STAY?

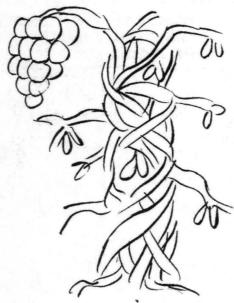

DOODLE MORE HEALTHY GRAPES GROWING FROM THE BRANCHES THAT ARE DI-VINE!

DOODLE WHAT CAN BE MADE FROM GREAT GRAPES!

NOT DIVINE! BE SILLY - WHAT CRAZY THINGS GROW ON THESE TREES?

The Crucifixion

DRAW A TIME YOU
EXPERIENCED ALMOST
UNBEARABLE PAIN.

CAN YOU DRAW THE SCENE ON CALVARY'S HILL?

THIS IS AN ACROSSTIC. WRITE OUT A WORD FOR EACH LETTER IN "JESUS" TO DESCRIBE HIM.

ANGER

DRAW A LITTLE PIECE OF PAPER AND A NAIL THROUGH IT... LEAVING IT AS A FORGIVEN SIN AT THE CROSS.

FINISH THE SCENE. WHAT DID MARY MAGDALENE FIND?

DOODLE JOHN OUTRUNNING PETER TO THE TOMB.

FACE IT!
DOODLE THE SHOCKED EXPRESSIONS OF PETER AND JOHN.

DRAW A RISEN JESUS
EASING MARY. WHAT'S HE SAYING?

CAN YOU SPELL OUT "APOSTLES"
WITH...HMM...YUM, YUM...BREAD CRUMBS!?

WOULD IT BUG YOU TO DOODLE REPENT-ANT?...
AND...WAIT FOR IT... PATIENT (PĀSH-ANT)?

OBD ANT (OBEDIENT)

Paul's Change

DRAW A BRIGHT LIGHT
FROM HEAVEN THAT MADE
SAUL FALL.

CAN YOU VISUALIZE A BRIGHT AND BLINDING LIGHT? DRAW IT!

GOD ASKED SAUL – WHO WOULD BE PAUL –
WHY HE WAS KICKING "AGAINST THE GOADS"
(WORKING AGAINST HIM). DOODLE SAUL KICKING
A GOAD.

KICKING GOAT

AFTER THE SCALES FELL OFF, SAUL
COULD SEE! DRAW AN ASTONISHED ANANIAS WHO JUST LAID
HANDS ON HIM.

WHOOPS - EPIC RIP CORD FAIL!

GOD HELPED US WHEN WE COULDN'T HELP OURSELVES.
DOODLE A WAY THIS GUY COULD BE HELPED.

DRAW THE UGLIEST SWAMP CRITTER
THAT LEAPS INTO YOUR MIND.

PICTURE YOURSELF RUNNING IN A RACE! WHAT OBSTACLES MIGHT YOU FACE?

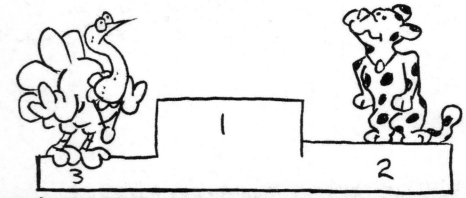

DRAW YOURSELF WINNING THE GOLD MEDAL!

HOLD IT RIGHT THERE!

DOODLE YOURSELF EXERCISING SELF-CONTROL!

DRAW AN AMAZING MAZE... AND OBSTACLES ALONG THE WAY.

WHAT IS THE RACE OF LIFE?

WHAT IS THE PRIZE?

TEMPTATION CAN FEEL LIKE SUCH A MONSTER.
DOODLE THIS BOY'S WAY OF ESCAPING.

DOODLE YOUR TEMPTATION MONSTER AND THE TOOL TO SLAY IT.

CARRY IT TO THE CROSS AND CARRY ON

WHAT CARES DO YOU NEED TO LAY DOWN AT THE FOOT OF THE CROSS?

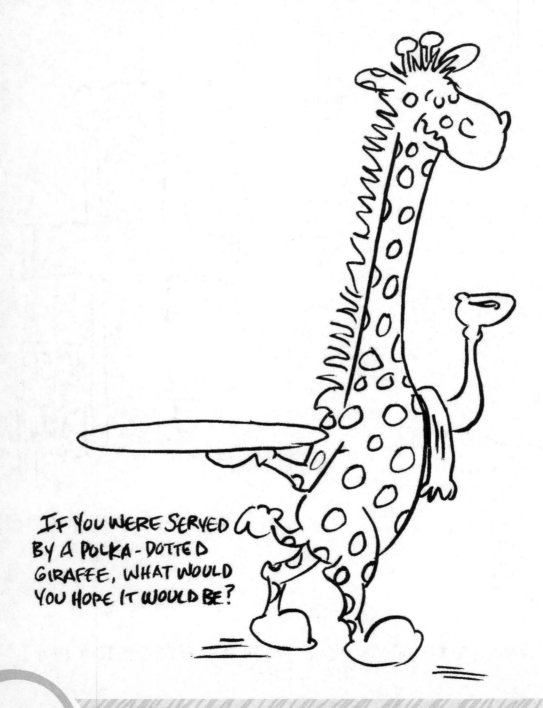

IF YOU WERE SERVED
BY A POLKA-DOTTED
GIRAFFE, WHAT WOULD
YOU HOPE IT WOULD BE?

WHICH FRUIT IS YOUR STRENGTH? PICTURE IT!

WHICH ONE IS YOUR
WEAKNESS? DRAW IT (AND DRAW NEAR TO GOD FOR HELP!).

BEAR ONE ANOTHER'S BURDENS. FINISH THESE BEARS. HOW ARE THEY HELPING EACH OTHER?

DOODLE HOW YOU CAN HELP SOMEONE WHO'S HAVING A PROBLEM... OR A 'BIRD'EN.

HOW CAN YOU HELP SOMEONE WHO'S FALLEN INTO THE QUICKSAND OF SIN?

WHAT LAW OF CHRIST DOES THIS FULFILL?

ENGRAVE IT!

NARROW WAY →

BROAD-WAY →

DOODLE SOMEONE RECEIVING THE GIFT OF GRACE.

DOODLE WAYS PEOPLE TRY TO EARN THEIR WAY TO HEAVEN.

IF I LEARN EVERY VERSE, I'LL MAKE IT THROUGH THE YOU-NI-VERSE!

SALVATION IS FREE? WHAT ABOUT SHIPPING AND HANDLING?

WHAT DOES FAITH LOOK LIKE?

Kindness

BEE WASN'T KIND. HIS WORDS STUNG. OUCH!

DOODLE A DIFFERENT KIND OF BEE... WITH WORDS SWEET AS HONEY!

BEE HAVE

WHO IS THIS TENDER HEART HELPING?

WHEN HAVE YOU FORGIVEN?

WHEN DID CHRIST FORGIVE YOU?

FINISH THE PICTURE OF THESE KIDS OBEYING OR HONORING MOM AND DAD... DOING A CHORE OR CELEBRATING A BIRTHDAY OR LISTENING TO A STORY.

THINK OF SOMETHING YOU HONOR.

PICTURE HONORING YOUR PARENTS.

WHAT IS THE PROMISE FOR HONORING YOUR PARENTS? FINISH THIS OLD MAN.

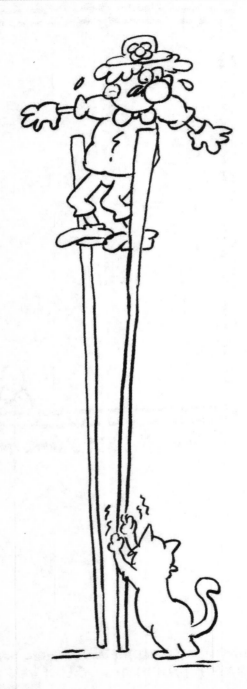

DOODLE WHAT CAUSES YOU TO BE ANXIOUS.

WHAT ATTITUDE GOES WITH PRAYER AND SUPPLICATION?

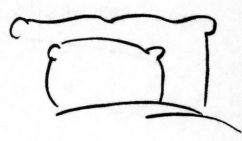

FINISH THIS THANKFUL GOBBLER.

DOODLE YOURSELF NEXT TO TEDDY LETTING YOUR REQUESTS BE MADE KNOWN TO GOD.

WHAT GUARDS OUR HEARTS AND MINDS IN CHRIST?

NO! NOT PIZZA OF GOD!

FINISH THIS AND ADD YUMMY TOPPINGS!

GOD EMPOWERS US TO DO UNBELIEVABLE THINGS.

DOODLE AN AMAZING PAINTING ON THE CEILING OF A BEAUTIFUL CATHEDRAL (CHURCH).

PICTURE A TIME WHEN GOD HAS GIVEN YOU STRENGTH.

IN WHAT WAY DO YOU NEED HIS HELP TODAY?

DOODLE OTHER ANIMALS WORKING HARD IN THE GARDEN. WHAT VEGGIES FOR THE TABLES ARE THEY GROWING?

CARROT TO DRAW?
LETTUCE SEE YOU DOODLE!

Day of the Lord

DOODLE WHAT IT MEANS TO BE "SONS OF LIGHT."

WAKE UP, SLEEPYHEAD!

ZORRO IN HIS SLEEP

ACCORDING TO VERSE SIX, WHAT COULD BE DONE INSTEAD?

DRAW YOU BEING COURAGEOUS IN THE MIDST OF THESE SITUATIONS.

TONIGHT'S SPEAKER: YOU!

DOODLE YOURSELF DEFENDING THIS VERY SCARY HAIRY BALLPLAYER.

HAIRYSVILLE SWEATY MEN

DOODLE THE MOST COURAGEOUS PERSON YOU KNOW.

DOODLE SOMEONE OR SOMETHING MAKING A SPECIAL APPEARANCE.

HOW DID JESUS MAKE A SPECIAL APPEARANCE? DOODLE IT!

BE ACRONIMBLE ... AND DOODLE A WORD FOR EACH LETTER THAT HELPS EXPLAIN THE ORIGINAL WORD.

GRACE

I
F
T

HOW CAN THIS ONE BE SAVED? HOW WERE YOU SAVED?

Restored

PAUL EXPRESSED HIS THANKS TO PHILEMON.
DOODLE WHO YOU ARE THANKFUL FOR TODAY.

PAUL WAS A PRISONER
IN CHAINS WHEN HE WROTE
THIS LETTER. IMAGINE THAT-
A CHAIN LETTER! DOODLE WHAT
ONESIMUS - THE RUNAWAY
SLAVE - LOOKED
LIKE. →

DOODLE ONESIMUS FACING HIS OLD MASTER.

WHAT DO YOU THINK PHILEMON SAID TO ONESIMUS?

ONESIMUS (WHICH MEANS "USEFUL") GOES BACK TO PHILEMON WITH A LETTER ASKING HIM TO BE RECEIVED AS PAUL, FORGIVEN AND PUT TO GOOD USE.

HAVE YOU EVER RUN AWAY?...
FROM YOUR HOME...SCHOOL...GOD? BABYSITTER?
HOW WERE YOU RESTORED? DOODLE IT!

Unchanging

THANKFULLY, WE HAVE AN UNCHANGING GOD. DOODLE A DIFFICULT CHANGE YOU'VE BEEN THROUGH IN YOUR LIFE.

DOODLE SOMETHING YOU DID YESTERDAY.

DOODLE SOMETHING YOU DID TODAY.

WRITE THINGS THAT DESCRIBE AN UN-CHANGING GOD.

DOODLE SOMETHING YOU'LL DO FOREVER.

DOORS OF THE WORD

(I HOPE YOU'RE OPEN TO THE PUN — DON'T KNOCK IT! ☺)

WHAT IS WRITTEN ON THE DOOR? (SCRIPTURE FROM THE WORD?)

WHO IS ENTERING? WHAT IS BEING DONE FOR THOSE ON THE OTHER SIDE?

THIS BOY IS HEARING THE WORD. NOW, HOW CAN HE BE DOING?

WHAT IS BEING SHARED?

WHO IS SHARING THE WORD?

Taming the Tongue

IT'S SMALL, BUT LIKE A FLAME, IT CAN LICK A FOREST.
DOODLE THE FOREST A FIRE.

DRAW
WHAT
YOUR
TONGUE
LICKS.

CAN ANYONE TAME THE WILD TONGUE?

FINISH THE TAMER.
WHERE IS THE WHIP?

DOODLE HOW A TONGUE CAN BE A BLESSING.

CAN YOU DOODLE BIG WORMS AT THE END OF HIS LINE SPELLING OUT THE WORD "CARES"?

HE CARROT FOR YOU.

WHAT EATS CARROTS?

FINISH THE BIG FISH, SPELLING OUT "JESUS" IN BUBBLE LETTERS. I **ALREADY** DID THE "U" AND "S". WHAT IS IT SWALLOWING?

DOODLE MORE SILLY CREATURES WALKING THE HIGH WIRE.

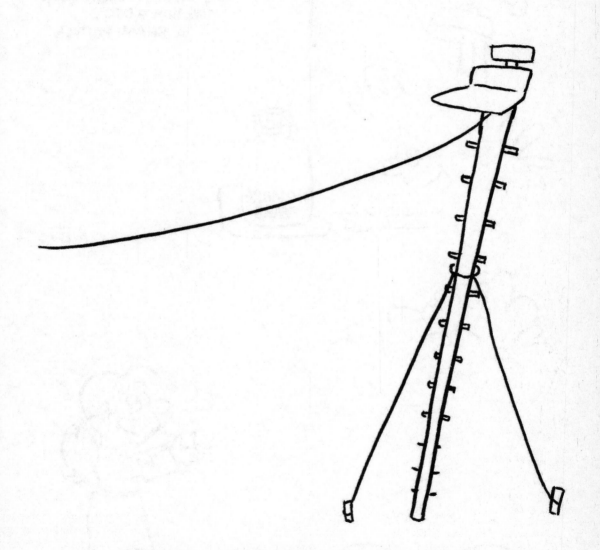

CAN YOU SPELL OUT "JESUS CATCHES ME" IN THE NET BELOW?

FINISH THIS SCENE.
SHOWER OF BLESSING?
IS THERE A RUBBER DUCKY?
THE BOY'S DOG?
A SHAM-POODLE?

NO MORE TEARS

PICTURE HEAVEN AND THIS GIRL GETTING HER TEARS WIPED AWAY.